The Complete Mastery Reading & Spelling Program™

Basic Code "My First Chapter Books"
Book 1

Matt's Pup

By Erin Brown Conroy, MA

Illustrations by Kate Flynn

Matt's Pup

ISBN: 978-0-9818488-3-9
Printed in the United States of America
©2009 by Erin Brown Conroy
All rights reserved

Cover and interior design by Isaac Publishing, Inc.

Library of Congress Cataloging-in-Publication Data°

IPI
Isaac Publishing, Inc.
P.O. 342
Three Rivers, MI 49093
www.isaacpublishing.com

No part of this book may be reproduced or transmitted in any form or by any means, electronic or mechanical—including photocopying, recording, or by any information storage and retrieval system—without permission in writing from the publisher, except as provided by United States of America copyright law.

Please direct your inquiries to admin@isaacpublishing.com

Testimonials for
The Complete Mastery Reading & Spelling Program™

"I started out with my four-year-old daughter with The Complete Mastery Reading & Spelling program—and in under six months, she tested at a grade 2.5 level of reading! Amazing!" – Mom to Odessa, in Kalamazoo, Michigan

"Because reading is so important, I wanted to make sure that my daughter started out reading right. Thank you so much – in four months' time, she went from knowing nothing to reading sentences—and enjoying reading—she thinks reading is fun! I recommend The Complete Mastery Reading & Spelling Program to anyone who wants to start their child out right." – Beth, an elementary School counselor and mom to a five-year-old daughter

"After just his first year in school, my son didn't want to read, and his teacher said that he needed help. Now—just two months later—Tristan is happy and smiling and reading words, and he can figure new words out easily. I've already told my friends about this program, because it changed our whole outlook on reading for us." –Michelle, mom to Tristan, age 6

"Two years ago, my son was reading at a second grade level. Today, because of The Complete Mastery Reading & Spelling Program, my son is reading and understanding high school and college reading! He didn't want to read at all—now he's excited. This program is phenomenal, and I recommend it to everyone because I know it works." – Denise, mom to William, age 12

"We spent 50 hours in a one-on-one nationally-known program with no success. The public schools were ready to put our 9-year-old son into special education. After only a few hours of working with The Complete Mastery Reading & Spelling Program, Victor's reading improved four levels within his grade, and his teacher was thrilled and amazed, as were we! I recommend the program to any parent who wants their child to read better." – Blake, dad to Victor

"Thank you so much! Because of CMRS, my daughter has become an enthusiastic learner. The program has made learning to read so much easier for her! All the manipulatives that are used have become an amazing game at our house…and the writing, marking of sounds, and games…reading has become fun! Our books are now marked with sound markings, making *the words easier to sound out. My daughter went from crying at the idea of reading to 'Can I go read a book?'—and she reads it for hours or until it is done! Thank you!"* – K. Durian, Michigan

"Thank you so much for CMRS! Morgan's spelling and reading are improving in only months. She has so much fun with the games. I don't think she realizes it's learning! We so appreciate it!" –Becky Callahan, Kalamazoo, Michigan

"Thank you! My son can now read! This is making home schooling so much easier! Everything is possible!" – Kim, Kalamazoo, Michigan

"I've seen Lavender improve her reading in a little over a month! And she is more confident!" – Annette, Kalamazoo, Michigan

"My son, Josiah, was not reading. He was really struggling to sound out even simple words. He had a lot of visual confusion and was just not getting it. I tried many phonics programs with him - we were both struggling through the materials and getting more and more discouraged. Then, with CMRS, learning to read became a pleasurable experience! We love the Sound Box concept and marking the words. Josiah is now reading—he is smoothly reading books…it's a world of difference for both of us. First, Josiah is learning to read in a way that fits his learning style – which has made it fun and given him a positive learning experience. For me, I have the needed tools to make Josiah's reading journey a success. We are grateful!" – J. Wing, Kalamazoo, Michigan

"Amazing! The games and marking the Sound Pictures make it fun—now my child can read any word, can sound out any word, and can spell better! Thank you!" – Martha Stanley, Kalamazoo, Michigan

"Every week, Austin's abilities and confidence toward reading has risen. He can break words down (decode), so now he can go through pages and read most of the words on his own, and he has confidence to attempt reading words he is unfamiliar with. Everything is in a concise order that was easily comprehended, and it has been wonderful to play the games. They made a huge impact on learning and retaining the sounds. Learning to read has been fun and successful!" – A grandmother teaching her grandson to read, Michigan

"The Complete Mastery Reading & Spelling Program is the best at helping my children learn in a fun and simple way. After trying phonics programs and not having success, I knew I had to try this one. This all-inclusive program began with learning the "basic code" and escalated into my children reading beyond my expectations. My daughter can read at a higher level! She can get excited about seeing words differently (in a good way)— and she can read confidently! Thank you, Erin, for designing a program that works!" – Jodi Carless, Kalamazoo, Michigan

"I've seen my fifth-grade son come a long ways—and because of reading better, we've seen a big improvement in his grades overall. He is able to figure out words on his own; he's able to read and understand the questions and content – which is something he couldn't do before. Now he reads five to seven pages a night and understands it all, and he feels better about it, too. Because of the reading, Social Studies wasn't a part of what he did at all; now, he is involved in advanced Social Studies!" – Mom to Tim, Allegan, Michigan

"I knew nothing about Sound Pieces. Reading was hard. I'm now reading books and newsletters on my own, where before, I wouldn't want to read at all. Before [The CMRS Program], I really didn't know how to read…now I can read! I like finding a good book. It's even fun to sit down and read a story! As I keep practicing what I've learned, I think I'll know how to read without mistakes, and that will really feel good!" – Tim, age 11, Allegan, Michigan

"Mikayla's self confidence has increased as she has been able to recognize Sound Pieces and put words together…her reading is improving so much that she's finally beginning to pick up books on her own, to read them. Her progress in reading is transferring into other areas of learning…It's clicking! Her excitement shows through…and her excitement shows the most when she can now pick up her Bible and read it—her main goal for learning how to read. Thank you!" – Wendy Stafford, Kalamazoo, Michigan

"We began with phonics for our son and we realized that he wasn't learning the same way that his sister had; the phonics that worked for her wasn't working for him. We looked at various reading programs, reading publisher & parent reviews. We decided to try a widely-publicized, "guaranteed" phonics program. It started out good, at least that's what I thought. It was fun, flashy, and he was reading words! The excitement was short lived. What he actually was doing was memorizing words. When he reached his memory capacity, he didn't understand how to break down new words and had a hard time reading words he had previously memorized from the program. He was getting frustrated because what he had been accomplishing wasn't working any more. I heard a lot of positive comments about The Complete Mastery Reading & Spelling Program, and Erin's experience with children. We started…and the progress he's made is amazing! He's gone from mastering the Basic Code to breaking down pretty big words for his age. He's retaining what he's learning. This program has made all the difference for him!" – A homeschooling mom, Kalamazoo, Michigan

"Fabulous!" – Mom in Kalamazoo, Michigan

"We enjoy the great games and 'playing' with sounds, to get familiar with them. My 3-year old at home loves to join in the learning, too!" – Mom in Michigan

"My daughter is learning this much quicker when we just tried to learn the letters. She's learning to read much sooner, as well!" – Mom in Michigan

"I enjoy the creativity in addressing difficult learning styles!" – Mom in Portage, Michigan

"I love how the children play games to learn!" – Diane, Kalamazoo, Michigan

"Wow! This reading way makes so much sense to me! A great way to learn the [Sound] Pieces!" – Amy, Richland, Michigan

"Thank you so much! Already, I'm seeing my son Jack experience successes with his reading!" – Maureen, a homeschooling Mom in Michigan

**The Complete Mastery
Reading & Spelling Program**™

Basic Code "My First Chapter Books"
Book 1

Matt's Pup

By Erin Brown Conroy, MA

Illustrations by Kate Flynn

Isaac Publishing
P.O. Box 342 Three Rivers, MI 49093 • 888.273.4JOY
www.isaacpublishing.com

Chapter 1
Matt's Pup has a Problem

Matt had a pup.
His pup was big, black,
and tan.
Matt felt his pup
was the best.

Once, Matt's pup
got mom's hat.
Mom had to mend it.

Once, Matt's pup ran
into the lamp.
Matt had to fix it.

Once, Matt's pup
got into the hot tub.
Dad had to jump in
and get him.
Dad, Mom, and Matt
were upset.
The pup was a problem.
Dad said, "The pup has to
get to a class."

Chapter 2
Matt's Pup at Class

At class, Matt's pup had to sit.
Matt's pup went
in and on
and up.
But the pup did not sit.
Matt went back.
Matt was sad.
"The pup will get it," Dad said.
"The pup will get it," Mom said.
Matt did not trust the pup
to get it.

Matt went to bed and slept.
At sunup,
Matt had a plan.
Matt had the pup
sit and sit
and sit.

The next class, Matt's pup did sit.
Matt felt glad.

At class, the pup had to stand.
Matt's pup went
in and on
and up.
But the pup did not stand.
Matt went back.
Matt was sad.

Matt had the pup
stand and stand
and stand.
The next class,
Matt's pup did stand.
Matt felt glad.
Dad, Mom, and Matt felt
the class was the best.

Chapter 3
The Contest

Matt's pal sent him a list.
The list said,
"The Best Pet Contest."
It said, "Pups and cats can win."
It said, "Pups can sit.
Pups can stand."
It said, "Cats can sit.
Cats can stand.
The best sit and stand wins."

Matt said, "Mom, Pup will win."
Matt said, "I will send pup
to the contest."
Mom said, "Lots of pups
will sit and stand."
Dad said, "Lots of pups
will sit and stand."
Matt said, "But Pup is the best."
"Yes," said Matt. "Pup will win."

Chapter 4
Will Matt's Pup Win?

Matt and his pup went
to the contest.
And Matt's Mom and Dad went.
Lots of pups and cats
were there.
Matt's pup felt glad.

Pup went in and on and up.

Matt said, "Sit!"

Did Matt's pup do it?

Yes! Matt's pup did sit!

Matt said, "Stand!"
Did Matt's pup do it?
Yes! Matt's pup did stand!
Many of the pups sat.
Some did not.
Some of the cats sat.
Many did not.
Will Matt's pup win?

Chapter 5
The Mess

It was the end of the contest.
The kids had to
stop and sit.
The pups and cats had to
stop and sit.
The moms and dads
sat next to the kids.
Dad, Mom, Matt, and Pup sat.

The man lifted his hand.
The man said, "The pups and cats were splendid!"
The man said, "And the kids were splendid!"
The man said, "But just one cat gets to win.
And just one pup
gets to win."

The man held up a gift.
The man said,
"The black cat wins!"
Clap! Clap! Clap!
The cats and pups were glad.
The cats and pups
went to jump up.
The moms, dads, and kids had to
get the cats and pups
back to a sit.

Matt's pup did not sit.
Matt's pup ran up and
onto the man!
The man fell!
The pups and cats went nuts!
The cats ran up.
The pups ran up.
Many pups and cats went up
and onto him.
It was a mess!

Matt's mom and dad had to
jump up to help.
Matt ran to get his pup.
Matt's pup went to
lick the man—yuck!
Matt felt bad.
Had his pup
ended the contest?

Chapter 6
The Win

Dad, Mom, and Matt
got Matt's pup back.
Matt's pup went next to Matt
to sulk.
Many pups and cats went back
to sit.
Were the dads and moms upset?
Was the man upset?

The man got up.
The man's hands went to
flatten his pants.
The man's hands went to
pick up the gift.
The man twisted the gift
in his hand.
The man held up
the last gift.

The moms, dads, and kids
held still.
The man's lips
went into a grin.
"A pup can't stand still,"
said the man.
Matt did not get it.
A pup can't stand still?

The man said,
"The big black and tan pup
did mess up pants.
But the black and tan pup
did not mess up his sit and stand
in the contest.
The black and tan pup wins!"

Matt's lips went into a grin.
Matt felt gladness
swell up into him.
The pup just had to jump up
and lick Matt.
"Matt's pup wins!" said the kids.
The dads and moms said, "Yes!
The pup wins!"

Dad was glad.
Dad had a big grin.
Mom was glad.
Mom had a big grin.
Matt was glad.
Matt had a big grin.
And Matt's pup had a big grin.

Parent/Teacher Notes

This book is your easy way to help your child successfully practice beginning reading skills. *Matt's Pup* has easy-to-blend, easy-to-read, simple, stepwise content that is sequential and straightforward. For no more "too-big words," no more hard-to-decipher "sight words" or long words, no more disinterest, no more frustration and discouragement. All of the words in *The CMRS Program's Basic Code Chapter Books*—including *Matt's Pup*—are 100%, totally-decodable words, easily read by beginning readers. The Basic Code Chapter Books help teach your child to read with simple, clear-cut text that's totally appropriate for your beginner reader.

Learning to read is a monumental task. Those of us who are already reading forget how much energy and thought that it takes, to learn to read. The following pages show what the child's mind is going through, to decode this simple book. By learning how to help your child identify and decode the words in this book, you will give your child the greatest gift that you can possibly give: the gift of future learning and growing, through reading.

How to use this book...

Parents, Teachers, Kids...Write in this book! In this book, your child will "find" and "mark" Sound Pictures.

What is a Sound Picture? A Sound Picture is any letter or group of letters representing a sound.

Why find and mark Sound Pictures?
In order to learn to read—and read *well*—children must learn to decode what's on the page by recognizing different letters or group of letters—the Sound Pictures—within words. First, "finding" and "marking" helps your child to learn the *process* of reading—the way to properly think regarding correct reading. Yes, there is a "right way"—a way that works completely—and "wrong way"—in the long run, a more difficult way—to think about and process reading. Those who learn to look within words for Sound Pictures—and who *know* the Sound Pictures—learn to read *faster, with smoothness, and with more comprehension*. Second, "finding" and "marking" simply helps your child practice correct reading. **The best way to mark Sound Pictures is with a pencil.** If a mistake is made when marking a

Sound Picture, the pencil mark can be easily erased.
Find one Sound Picture at a time. At the beginning of reading with The CMRS Program™, we teach the children to find all of the Sound Pictures on a single page BEFORE reading the page. (Parent/Teacher: "Do you see the word "the" on the page?" Parent/teacher shows the child a card with the word, "the." "Let's find the word, 'the' and circle it.") When a child has some level of mastery of the Sound Pictures, he/she can read and mark at the same time. Then, when reading, the child knows which words to "sound out" and which words are Memory Words. In the same way, your child can find all of the separate sounds and their Sound Pictures, to make the reading eariser to decode and read through.

In this book, you will find and mark...

Doubles
What is a "Double"? A Double consists of two letters side-by-side that are the exact same—and are spoken as one sound. For example, the name "Matt" has to t's at the end...but when we read the name, "Matt," we do not say both t's. We only say one /t/ sound.
How are Doubles marked? Doubles are underlined.
Doubles found in this book: tt (Matt, Matt's, flatten), ss (class, mess, gladness), ll (will, swell, fell, still)

The Basic Code "ck" and "qu"
What's so "special" about the "ck" and "qu"? In The CMRS Program's Basic Code™, there are two letter groupings that are identified as "going together": "ck" and "qu." Children learn that the /k/ sound is drawn three ways: c, k, and ck. Children also learn that the /kw/ sound is drawn with two letters, not just one (In English, the "u" always follows the "q"). In order to "see" the "ck" and "qu" as letters grouped together, we draw a box around the "ck" and "qu" letters.
NOTE: There are two letters in the Basic Code that have two sounds: x (/ks/) and qu (/kw/). All other Basic Code letters have one sound per picture.
Words with the "ck" and "qu" sounds found in this book: *black, back, lick, yuck*

The Basic Code "Buzz 's'"
What is a "Buzz 's'"? In English, the letter "s" is frequently representative of the /z/ sound (as in the word, "kids"). In The CMRS Program™, the Buzz "s" is included in The Basic Code; children learn the Buzz "s" at the same time that they learn the /z/ Sound Picture.
How is the Buzz "s" marked? The Buzz "s" has a squiggly zig-zag line underneath the "s." NOTE: The Buzz "s" is almost always found at the ends of words.
Buzz "s" Sound Pictures found in this book: *mom's, wins, dads, kids, hands*
"Buzz Words" (high-frequency use of the Buzz "s"): *is, his, as, has, was*

Blends
What is a "Blend"? A Blend is also called a "consonant blend." A consonant blend is made up of two or three consonants that are placed next to each other. A consonant is any single letter that isn't a vowel (a-e-i-o-u). Each consonant represents one sound in The Basic Code… and each letter in the Blend is spoken, or voiced. For example, with the "st" Blend, both the "s" and the "t" are sounds that are voiced. In The CMRS Program™, children purposefully learn—and, through workbooks, games, and fun—practice every single one of the 49 two- and three-letter beginning and ending Blends of the English language
How are Blends marked? The Blend is marked with a gray shade, covering over the two or three Blend letters. You can simply color over the letters of the blend with a pencil.
Blends found in this book: *pr, bl, nd, lt, st, mp, cl, nt, tr, sl, pt, pl, xt, gl, spl, ld, lk. ft, ts, tw, gr, and sw.*

Memory Words
What is a "Memory Word"? Memory Words are words in the English language that cannot be "sounded out" and must be memorized as "whole pictures"; the entire word is seen and read as one unit.
Are Memory Words the same as Sight Words? No. Memory Words are not the same as the "sight words" of phonics. Phonics lists sometimes have over one-hundred "sight words." Because *The Complete Mastery Reading & Spelling Program*™ more completely decodes the English language, with The CMRS Program™, there are only a handful of Memory Words to memorize.

How are Memory Words marked? Most Memory Words are marked by circling the entire word. The Memory Word "a" (pronounced "uh"—the same as the vowel /u/ as in "hug") is marked by drawing a u-shape under the letter "a." NOTE: There is no word called "a" (pronounced "ay"); when the letter "a" is alone, as in the representation of the word (a pup, a cat, etc.), the word is pronounced "uh."

Memory Words found in this book: *a, the, once, of, were, there, and one*

Marked Memory Words

What is a "Marked Memory Word"? A Marked Memory Word is a word that *can* be "sounded out" within The CMRS Program™ (even though other methods call these words "sight words" that, in their methodology, cannot be "sounded out"). However, the Sound Pictures found within Marked Memory Words are advanced Sound Pictures—learned in the upper levels of the program. Because most of the books and reading materials available for children today use certain words with advanced pieces, we have chosen to include the Marked Memory Words in our materials—marked with the advanced Sound Pictures. Then your child can read non-CMRS books well, also.

How are Marked Memory Words marked?

To, into, onto, **and** *do* are marked with two small circles over the "o" in each word.

Said **and** *many* are marked with a small letter "e" over the "ai" in "said" and the "a" in "many."

Many is also marked with a small capital "E" drawn within the center of the "y."

Some is marked with a "u" shape under to "o" and an underline under the "me"; then cross out the "e."

Parents and Teachers—

The following pages are your "key"—so that you can help your child/student to find and mark the Sound Pictures. Enjoy the time with your child—and enjoy the process of learning to read!

Parent/Teacher Key

Chapter 1
Matt's Pup has a Problem

Matt had a pup.
His pup was big, black,
and tan.
Matt felt his pup
was the best.
Once, Matt's pup
got mom's hat.
Mom had to mend it.
Once, Matt's pup ran
into the lamp.
Matt had to fix it.
Once, Matt's pup
got into the hot tub.
Dad had to jump in
and get him.
Dad, Mom, and Matt
were upset.
The pup was a problem.
Dad said, "The pup has to
get to a class."

Chapter 2
Matt's Pup at Class

At class, Matt's pup had to sit.
Matt's pup went
in and on
and up.
But the pup did not sit.
Matt went back.
Matt was sad.
"The pup will get it," Dad said.
"The pup will get it," Mom said.
Matt did not trust the pup
to get it.
Matt went to bed and slept.
At sunup,
Matt had a plan.
Matt had the pup
sit and sit
and sit.
The next class, Matt's pup did sit.
Matt felt glad.
At class, the pup had to stand.
Matt's pup went
in and on
and up.
But the pup did not stand.
Matt went back.
Matt was sad.

Chapter 2 Cont'd

Matt had the pup
stand and stand
and stand.
The next class,
Matt's pup did stand.
Matt felt glad.
Dad, Mom, and Matt felt
the class was the best.

Chapter 3
The Contest

Matt's pal sent him a list.
The list said,
"The Best Pet Contest."
It said, "Pups and cats can win."
It said, "Pups can sit.
Pups can stand."
It said, "Cats can sit.
Cats can stand."
The best sit and stand wins.
Matt said, "Mom, Pup will win."
Matt said, "I will send pup
to the contest."
Mom said, "Lots of pups
will sit and stand."
Dad said, "Lots of pups
will sit and stand."
Matt said, "But Pup is the best."
"Yes," said Matt. "Pup will win."

Chapter 4
Will Matt's Pup Win?

Matt and his pup went
to the contest.
And Matt's Mom and Dad went.
Lots of pups and cats
were there.
Matt's pup felt glad.

Pup went in and on and up.
Matt said, "Sit!"
Did Matt's pup do it?
Yes! Matt's pup did sit!

Matt said, "Stand!"
Did Matt's pup do it?
Yes! Matt's pup did stand!
Many of the pups sat.
Some did not.
Some of the cats sat.
Many did not.
Will Matt's pup win?

Chapter 5
The Mess

It was the end of the contest.
The kids had to
stop and sit.
The pups and cats had to
stop and sit.
The moms and dads
sat next to the kids.
Dad, Mom, Matt, and Pup sat.
The man lifted his hands.
The man said, "The pups and cats
were splendid!"
The man said, "And the kids
were splendid!"
The man said, "But just one cat
gets to win.
And just one pup
gets to win."
The man held up a gift.
The man said,
"The black cat wins!"
Clap! Clap! Clap!
The cats and pups were glad.
The cats and pups
went to jump up.
The moms, dads, and kids had to
get the cats and pups
back to a sit.

Matt's pup did not sit.
Matt's pup ran up and
onto the man!
The man fell!
The pups and cats went nuts!
The cats ran up.
The pups ran up.
Many pups and cats went up
and onto him.
It was a mess!
Matt's mom and dad had to
jump up to help.
Matt ran to get his pup.
Matt's pup went to
lick the man—yuck!
Matt felt bad.
Had his pup
ended the contest?

Chapter 6
The Win

Dad, Mom, and Matt
got Matt's pup back.
Matt's pup went next to Matt
to sulk.
Many pups and cats went back
to sit.
Were the dads and moms upset?
Was the man upset?

The man got up.
The man's hands went to
flatten his pants.
The man's hands went to
pick up the gift.
The man twisted the gift
in his hand.
The man held up
the last gift.

The moms, dads, and kids
held still.
The man's lips
went into a grin.
"A pup can't stand still,"
said the man.
Matt did not get it.
A pup can't stand still?

The man said,
"The big black and tan pup
did mess up pants.
But the black and tan pup
did not mess up his sit and stand
in the contest.
The black and tan pup wins!"
Matt's lips went into a grin.
Matt felt gladness
swell up into him.
The pup just had to jump up
and lick Matt.
"Matt's pup wins!" said the kids.
The dads and moms said, "Yes!
The pup wins!"

Dad was glad.
Dad had a big grin.
Mom was glad.
Mom had a big grin.
Matt was glad.
Matt had a big grin.
And Matt's pup had a big grin.

The next 10 seconds of reading this page could change your life…

Who Else Wants To Absolutely Get Your Child to Master Reading—and Even Jump Two Grade Levels of Reading in One Year?

Since you've picked up and flipped through lots of books before like you're doing now, you're probably ready to put the book down and walk on. But **wait one second** before you do it.

Imagine having your child come up to you—**excited** about reading, **a smile** on the face, **sparkles** in the eyes, **hugging** the book **with delight** because the two of you are ready to sit down and enjoy reading together. **You feel good** because you have given your child **all** of the learning tools needed—and your child is now **reading fast, smoothly, and with 100% comprehension.**

It's true: This story can be you.

Reading this page—and holding this book—can be different than any other book out there— Because **you now have in your hand what can be the beginning of your child learning to read with Complete Mastery Reading & Spelling.**

You can **have your child not miss a thing**, when it comes to learning to read—by resting in the fact that you're **giving your child the most comprehensive, solid start in reading**—*today.*

I'm guessing that you're like me in that **you feel like you absolutely must give your child the most rock-solid start in life that's possible**—in so many things, but **especially in reading**—because reading will **positively impact your child's entire life!** (Isn't that true?)

So what we do, to **make it happen *now?***

Here's the answer:

- Find out about—and get going with—The Complete Mastery Reading & Spelling Program™ today. This book is only the beginning—just a small part of a great-big program brimming with benefits for your child. Books, DVDs, classes—it's all on the horizon.

Visit www.ReadWithCMRS.com Call 1-888-303-5757. Get your child moving into the best direction possible for reading, *right now.*

- **As a part of a group of people who want to positively impact the future of your children**—and, truly, children *everywhere*—then contact Erin Brown Conroy, MA, child specialist, 30-year educator, author, and passionate mom with 13 children who cares about the future just like you—and **bring Erin to speak to your group** about how you can dynamically make a difference in a child's life through the hope of reading. **Bring Erin in. Email erin@erinbrown.conroy.com. Pick up the phone and call 259-207-0397.** Get an experience that **saves you time** in getting your child to faster reading, **saves you money** in buying the "right" books that will truly help your child successfully read, and, quite possibly, **saves a child** you know from a bleak future without the benefit of highly-skilled reading and all the benefits of learning—not just in school but in *life*—that are attached to reading well.

- **Moms, Dads, Homeschool Parents, Teachers**—If you're a person who passionately cares about teaching kids, then **find out about Certified Instructor Training for The Complete Mastery Reading & Spelling Program**™. You can be trained in a way that you can change lives—to **make a difference** as you bring skill and ability to your child, to other children, while you bring high self-esteem…bring hope…bring confidence…and, in reality, bring a future. **Be a part of the new, multi-sensory, learning-style sensitive, totally decodable, enjoyable and easy-to-remember way to learn to read.** Bringing skills to children everywhere, watching kids get fired-up about reading—and mastering reading completely. **Call 1-888-303-5757** and get more info today.

Whether it's for your child or for someone you know—
Don't you agree?…It's time to find out more about
The Complete Mastery Reading & Spelling Program™

www.ReadWithCMRS.com
1-888-303-5757

Warmly wishing you all the best,

Erin Brown Conroy
author, CMRS creator

www.ingramcontent.com/pod-product-compliance
Lightning Source LLC
Chambersburg PA
CBHW071409040426
42444CB00009B/2171